TEACHINGS
ON THE
NATURE
OF
MIND

Lama Ole Nydahl

Blue Dolphin Publishing
1993

His Holiness the 16th Gyalwa Karmapa

Copyright © 1993 Ole Nydahl
All rights reserved.

For further information, address
Blue Dolphin Publishing, Inc.
P.O. Box 1908, Nevada City, CA 95959

ISBN: 0-931892-58-9

Printed in the United States of America by
Blue Dolphin Press, Inc., Grass Valley, California

5 4 3 2 1

FOREWORD

My students keep getting brighter, so it is again time for more comprehensive teachings.

A lecture at the Sakyamuni Buddha center in Canberra, Australia, in March '91 offered the raw material for this booklet. Liliana Zapata and Fernando Cifuentes supported its financing, Helen and Angela of Sydney improved my English, and Paul, Tomek, Katherine and Roland helped with the fine points. Edita and Andreas of Hamburg offered precious hours of their honeymoon for writing it down. This time Caty distracted us most.

May we soon have a Karmapa all can trust.

Mahakala day of Mahakala Week,
February, 1993
Frazer Island, Australia

Hannah and Ole Nydahl

Lama Ole Nydahl

TEACHINGS ON THE NATURE OF MIND

How Buddhism transcends cultural concepts

It is difficult to imagine a better teaching situation than the one the Buddha enjoyed 2,550 years ago, with highly intelligent students and forty-five years of sharing his enlightenment. Therefore, the teachings are exceedingly vast. The *Kanjur,* the Buddha's direct words, consists of 108 volumes containing 84,000 helpful teachings, and the later commentaries — *Tenjur* — comprise another 254 inch-thick books. His last words highlight this fact: "I can die happily, I have not kept a single teaching in a closed hand. Whatever can benefit you, I have already given."

As Buddhism contains such a richness of material, defining it only by what it is can be confusing. Also knowing what it is not will bring out its masterly contours, and this is a good way to start. We should be aware that it is extremely practical. When people asked the Buddha why and what he taught, his reply was always the same, very simple and direct: "I teach because you and all beings want to be happy and avoid suffering. I teach the way things are."

Every time somebody has tried to make these teachings conform to a system, it has not been large enough. For instance, many people say that Buddhism is a philosophy. This is true in the sense that Buddhism is logical. Mental clarity is the expression of insight and appears naturally through our development. As Buddhism makes emotional, inspirational, associative, intuitive and logical aspects of mind all grow together, then why can we not call it a philosophy?

Because it changes us. Philosophy is something we work with outside and on the level of ideas. Then we put the book back on the shelf. Here Buddhism is different. It touches our totality, and in a lasting way. Because the teachings give the key to what happens inside and around us every day, they alter us. We are not the same when we have used them.

Others have singled out this transformative effect and therefore claim it is a psychology. What shall we say to that? The goal of psychology is clear. All schools aim to keep us productive and not too difficult for others or ourselves during the sixty to eighty years most are here.

Buddhism continues on from here. It was given to bring bliss, inspiration and insight without end—to make all richness arise continually in the mind. Producing a state where subject, object and action are no longer experienced as separate, that jovial, non-dual condition permits all the perfect qualities of the mind to naturally express themselves. Though both psychology and Buddhism change us, psychology leads to the point where Buddhism starts. The goal of Buddhism is always absolute. It aims beyond duality to a state of oneness.

Finally some claim that Buddhism is actually a religion. Here one should first ask what they understand by that word. It actually consists of Latin *re* meaning "again," and *ligare,* meaning "to unite." Religion means re-union. But there is nothing to re-unite in Buddhism. There is no paradise we fell out of. A Buddhist could not trust that. If we had been in some kind of a perfect state and then lost it, the state would not be perfect, and we might fall out again.

Also, Buddhism is not "New Age," where a new truth is suddenly brought forth. We can trust that even less. If something appears at a certain time and place, it must be conditioned. Arising from several factors, it will change and surely disappear.

What, then, does the Buddha teach? He tells us that there is an underlying essence, a truth that has never been created or made. It is timeless and all-pervading, but can be understood and recognized from a certain position and time. He calls this timeless essence the nature of truth, or Dharmakaya. It is everywhere and always: the question is only when we recognize it.

It is also a relief that he disclaims any creating, judging or punishing god. He shows the world to be our collective dream. We ourselves create it. It appears from our collective subconsciousness. Through our accumulated actions (Karma), situations appear, and we are born into different bodies and places. The Buddha himself is a teacher, example and friend. He shows us how things function. Thus, we can have the happiness we want and avoid the suffering which nobody likes.

So what is Buddhism? The best word to describe his teaching is a word the Buddha himself chose. He called it Dharma. The Tibetan term is *Choe*. It means "the way things are." When we know how things work, we can do, think and say what is intelligent and joy-bringing, avoiding at the same time what brings harm. Helping us live, die and be reborn better: this is his goal.

History of Buddha: Background and Youth

A look at the Buddha's situation makes his teaching come alive. He was born into a royal family about 2,580 years ago and may have looked like some of you reading this: The texts say that his eyes were blue. His family's estate was around a village called Lumbini, lying in Nepal just across from the Indian border. He was his mother's last chance to give birth, and when he was born, three wise men were called to examine him. They all told his parents this: "The boy is special. If he is not confronted with the suffering of the world, he will become everything you want. A strong king, he will conquer the neighboring kingdoms and fulfill all your ambitions. If, on the other hand, he recognizes the unsatisfactory nature of all conditioned existence, he will abandon everything and ultimately bring new dimensions into the world."

Being like parents everywhere, they thought: we know what we have, but we don't know what we may get. So they decided to play it safe. Right from the beginning of his life, they succeeded in keeping the young prince surrounded by anything a healthy young man likes: exquisite women, sports, excitements of many kinds and a chance for intellectual pursuits. Any joy he wanted, he just needed to point to. This was his life until he became twenty-nine and experienced the things that burst the bubble and turned his world on its head.

His disillusionment

During three consecutive days, he was confronted with somebody sick, old and dead. Understanding that this happens to everyone, his whole set of values were destroyed. Back at his castle, he had a bad night. It was impossible to find something that one can really rely on. Wherever he looked, inside or out, he saw impermanence. There was nothing that can endure, nothing that has any lasting nature. No thing was really, truly there.

The fourth morning he passed a yogi, seated in deep meditation. Seeing him, he realized that this was what he searched for. This man experienced something timeless. He did not only see the thoughts and feelings inside and the situations and worlds outside. He also experienced the open space which makes everything possible and knows the radiant clarity which brings forth the unlimited nature of it all. He was the ocean, not only the waves; the mirror and experiencer more than the pictures and experiences. This second quality, unmoving, unchanging awareness, the prince recognized as the timeless essence he was looking for. He knew he had found that on which all can rely.

At that time, there were no teachings of the kind we today call Mahamudra or Maha-Ati, Chag-Chen or Dzog-Chen. They were only given by the Buddha after his enlightenment. There was no way known to directly recognize mind while brushing one's teeth, eating, sleeping, making love or whatever. Methods using all things to mirror the mind did not yet exist. So instead of working with his full life-situation, being aware in it all, he had to withdraw from everything. There was no alternative to limiting the amount of input reaching his mind. . . . Cutting off his rich private and public life, he went to the hills and forests of northern India to meditate.

Six intensive years followed, and he did not make things easy on himself. Wanting enlightenment more than anything, he used any method received to the hilt. Once, holding the dualistic view that the body is bad, he fasted himself to nearly a skeleton. He thought that diminishing sense-impressions would improve his clarity of mind, but discovered instead that from a weak position he could benefit neither others, nor himself. He then resumed eating and treating his body normally.

He learned from the main teachers of his time and usually surpassed them quickly. They all knew many things about events in the mind but not about its nature. Having perfected all their systems and ideas, he again found nothing solid to rely on.

The Buddha's Time

The Buddha's time was one of unprecedented mental activity. At certain places and times, such as ancient Greece, during the Renaissance, and even our own 1960s, the human mind has been especially shiny and aware. Though we lost much of a generation to chemicals, people were open and dreamed of building a meaningful life. They had deep idealism and confidence in the mind without being too snobbish or materialistic. The Buddha's situation may have had less warmth and informality than today, but was more quality-conscious concerning the stringency of logic. All the schools of philosophy known today existed even at that time. Materialism, nihilism, idealism, transcendentalism, existentialism: they were all there, and people expected them to touch their lives in a practical way.

It was not like our Western history, where a professor somewhere in Germany comes up with a thesis, some young artists are inspired and people start writing poems and building windows in a new way. Then, fifty years later, another professor produces another view, and again the poems and windows change.

In the Buddha's time people wanted more. A philosophy was expected both to present a transpersonal view of the world to be lasting, and to contain a practice. The teachings had to have a basis, present a way to follow, and bring about an attainable goal. People also had to be careful about what they said. If one presented a thesis and someone else disproved it, intellectual honesty at that time demanded that one became that person's student.

After six years spent like this in the lowlands of northern India, he came to a place which is today called Bodh-Gaya. It lies about two-thirds of the way from Delhi to Calcutta, in the now hopelessly overpopulated state of Bihar. Arriving there, the promises he had built up during many lives awakened. Sitting down, he vowed to meditate there until he really understood how things function and had the powers to benefit all beings.

He stayed in deep absorption for six days and six nights. On the morning of the seventh day, both his thirty-fifth birthday and the same day on which he later died, on this full moon morning in the month of May, all veils of confusion and separation dissolved. All notions of separation between the space and energy in himself and all things were gone, and his mind became awareness, conscious space, unlimited by past, present, and future. Through every atom, he knew and was everything.

During the first three weeks after reaching the goal, the Buddha remained in Bodh-Gaya. Here many gods came to him for blessing and refuge. The first teaching to humans he gave seven weeks after his enlightenment, at a place called Sarnath. It lies eleven km from Benares, where the Hindus burn their dead. There he met a group of people we would today call egotists—the humorless kind I always send elsewhere. Their main aim was to avoid their own problems, to remove their suffering.

They had been impressed by him while he practiced austerities. When he started treating his body in a healthy way, however, they considered him very unspiritual and left. Now that they met him again, at first they resolved to ignore him. When they came closer, however, and felt his radiant energy field, they had no choice. "What happened to you?" they asked. "How did you become like this?"

Four Noble Truths

His reply to them was that he had understood the "Four Noble Truths." Though they contain everything, they were given in a way to especially benefit those who think only of themselves.

His first statement was: *"There is suffering."* When people hear this, many think: "What kind of pessimism is this?" or: "How will he sell that?" Other religions are more inspiring. They say, "My God is stronger than yours," or "Allah's revenge is merciless and without fail"—something to make people feel part of something great.

Actually, this first statement is exceedingly vast. What most forget is that everything is relative, that all experience depends on the context in which it occurs. People surely don't need a Buddha to tell them there are happy and unhappy days. During my twenty years of giving interviews so far, I have seen that all beings are very aware of how they feel, regardless of intelligence. Instead, people need a Buddha to teach them what they don't know. Without him, they will miss the absolute level, the view of highest joy from the position of enlightenment.

This is what the Buddha means. "There is suffering" simply expresses that, compared to the bliss of enlightenment, to the experience of the open and limitless essence of mind, EVERYTHING is suffering. Even the highest moment of fearless joy and love, the most fulfilling excitement, the deepest absorptions: all are less perfect than our constant state when enlightenment has been realized. That is why the Buddha's first noble truth is not putting us down. It lifts us up. Saying that our true nature is better than anything we know today, he makes us rich.

His second statement was: *"Suffering has a cause."* And of what kind? The Buddha here points to mind's basic ignorance, to its inability to know that the seer, the things seen, and the act of seeing are aspects of the same totality. The mind of an unenlightened being functions like an eye. It sees anything happening, but it cannot see itself. We can be aware of so many things. We can establish the color, size, weight, smell, and form of everything in the world. But if I ask you to supply the same characteristics about your mind, you cannot do that. We know everything about phenomena, but very little about whatever experiences them. This very inability of mind to experience itself is the root of the conditioned world, the cause of all suffering.

Due to this limited power of experience, duality appears. The essence of our mind, its "space," then experiences itself as an "I." What appears in that space becomes "something else," a "you" or "the world outside." Though everything is conditioned, changing and not lastingly or truly "there," still we think it is real. From the separation felt between an "I" and a "you," between a here and a there, between this and that, the main disturbing feelings—attachment, aversion and confusion—will naturally appear. From attachment springs greed: what we like, we want to keep. From aversion comes envy, because the ones we don't like, we don't want to see happy. And from confusion appears the bad, exclusive kind of pride. The good one is the recognition that we are all essentially Buddhas, but when the bad one strikes, we think we exist as a "somebody" that could be better than others. We are then not aware that everything appears, dissolves and disappears, having no solid basis or content.

These six basic disturbing feelings, arising from ignorance about the nature of mind, then enter into 84,000 possible combinations. Though they change all the time, and can really be compared to a strange-looking zoo walking by, still we believe each of these animals exist. We fail to see that they were not there before, that they will not be there later, that right now they change all the time, and that we would be stupid to follow them. Instead, we react to them with body, speech and mind, sowing seeds of confusion in our subconscious and in the world outside. The result can only be later troubles. Depressions and outer obstacles will appear, and when this happens, we habitually consider them the fault of others. We forget we planted the seeds ourselves. So once again we feel motivated to do, think and say something harmful, which will once more sow future problems. This is why the Buddha explains ignorance to be the cause of suffering. The reason is simply that beings do not experience their true nature.

The Buddha's third statement at that historic meeting 2,550 years ago is wonderful, nothing less than that. He affirms that there is an *"end to suffering,"* a perfect state. He, himself, is this truth, and from then on he ceaselessly manifests the ultimate, true and timeless nature of mind.

Mind in its essence is radiant awareness, is clear space. Its true nature is the experience of greatest joy. Without wanting to, it expresses active compassion. Its pacifying, enriching, fascinating, and powerfully protective activities arise spontaneously, without any concept of anybody doing anything to anybody. They appear naturally, the way the sun shines. Our neuroses or uncontrolled inner states, "sins" in the terminology of other religions, are also no problem. They should be seen as the raw material for enlightenment. By being aware of them, without reacting, by seeing them as the free play of the mind, corresponding wisdoms appear.

When our anger is transformed, the resultant insight is clear like a mirror. It neither adds nor withdraws anything. Our pride returns as a recognition of the composite nature of all things. Our attachment becomes the ability to see situations both singly and as parts of a totality. Our jealousy—already now expert at thinking ahead and back—manifests the wisdom of experience, and even our confusion reappears as all-pervading intuition.

This is how the Buddha manifests the goal. He confirms that these three qualities, four activities and five wisdoms are everybody's true nature. The only difference between him and us, he says, is that he did the work necessary to perfect them, and we haven't done it yet.

His fourth and last statement is: *"There is a way that leads to the ending of suffering."* It consists of timelessly effective means for working with body, speech and mind. He taught these methods continually from the age of 35, when he manifested enlightenment, to the age of 80, when he left his body. For a full 45 years, surrounded by frequently very exciting and bright people, he taught the 84,000 teachings that can benefit all.

The Great Way

Eight years after his enlightenment, a very different group came to meet him at Rajgir, a mountaintop some hours by bus from Bodh-Gaya. These had natural warmth and compassion, a wide non-personal view, and much surplus energy for others. There, the Buddha based his teaching on these qualities, showing them how to strengthen compassion until subject, object and action were no longer separate. He also gave their natural wisdom a hand, helping them see what is, and not what they hoped or feared might be. As always, he insisted that these two qualities—compassion and wisdom—be balanced and develop together, that they be like legs and eyes. Compassion alone would otherwise become sentimental and dogmatic, while wisdom alone is cold, bureaucratic and life-defeating. One needs both to arrive.

Compassion

On the first level of compassion, we "like" people when they behave as we expect. I'm sure we all have that one. The second stage is when we also wish people well if they make mistakes or are difficult. We understand that their main motivation is not evil, but stupidity. They want happiness like everyone else, but not knowing what brings it about, they cause suffering instead. Out of ignorance, they put their hands into the nettles instead of the flowers.

The third kind of compassion is beyond anything personal. It is like the sun which simply shines. It does not decide that Mr. Jones is a bad man, that he should get the cancer rays, while kind Mr. Smith should get the tanning ones instead. The people, themselves, choose what they want. This non-discriminating compassion, going beyond all limitations, is absolute. The first two kinds can be compared to projecting nice pictures onto the mirror of the mind, but the third is the radiance of the mirror itself. When that has been recognized, it is timeless.

Wisdom: Liberation and Enlightenment

There are two kinds of wisdom: that which concerns the things happening in the mind, and the kind which knows mind itself. The first we learn in schools and universities. It enables us to have interesting jobs, earn good money, drive fast cars and die with more debt than our neighbor. It is very fine, but when they put us in the grave, all benefit is gone. This wisdom is limited to things that we cannot take with us. "The last shirt has no pockets," as the Danes say.

Insight into the nature of mind, on the other hand, can never be lost. Mind is open, clear and limitless like space—it has never been born and can never die. For that reason, whichever of its aspects we realize, they are of a permanent nature and will benefit us from life to life.

How, then, does mind recognize itself? Through adding more ideas and thoughts? No! Removing concepts is the way. Even the monks, usually of the Gelugpa lineage, who spend days in heated debate, cannot add anything to the truth-nature of mind. By being awareness itself and seeing whatever happens as its free play, we calm and transcend mind's fabricating tendency. Thus true and intuitive understanding will arise, and we recognize things both as they are and as they appear to be.

What keeps ordinary people from seeing what is really there? If we look, the culprits are two veils. The first veil is disturbing emotions, changing states of mind. If we change too strongly between happiness and suffering, between likes and dislikes, we shall not see much of what is really going on. The second veil is stiff ideas, the tendency to think that the finger pointing *is* the moon, that the word or concept *is* the experience, which of course they are not.

We need to remove both veils. Disturbing feelings appear because of mind's inability to recognize its nature as space: open, clear and limitless. Unable to understand itself as existing in all times and places, and encompassing all things, the mind feels separation, and disturbing feelings arise.

As long as we think "we," everything fits. When the feeling arises of a "me" here and a "you" there, trouble starts. Then attachment arises for what we want, and ill-will against what we don't like. From these basic feelings, a range of 84,000 conditioned states of mind may appear. Thus it is a great liberation that there exists no true "self," ego or "I"; that there is no "person" anywhere. This most important recognition follows two steps: first, we see that there is no self or "I" in the body, only a lot of moving atoms. There is also no "I" or self in our thoughts and feelings. Though we find streams of experiences which may be felt to be real, they do not remain.

Gradually, a total reaction to this understanding follows: If the true nature of mind is space, clear and limitless, how can we be hurt? What can disturb space? Recognizing that there is no self, we can no longer be the target. We no longer feel we're being shot at. Instead of "I am suffering," our reaction to pain will be: "There exists suffering." We become aware that beings want happiness but do unskillful things, and we work to avoid that.

Thus disappears the first veil, the one of mixed feelings. The result is "liberation," a state where one cannot suffer any more. This is the aim of the "southern" Buddhist schools and is mainly useful only for ourselves. If we want to benefit others, however, our way must continue from liberation on to enlightenment. Starting from the insight that our true essence cannot be harmed or hurt, we must move on to the full development of our mind. Its all-knowingness, spontaneous joy and active compassion is the absolute goal. These are always our true essence and appear when we remove mind's second veil, that of stiff ideas.

Though it is not easy to understand from daily-life situations that only mind is real, that it is radiant space which is now looking through our eyes and listening through our ears, there is no alternative, and we must try. Everything else—every thought and feeling, every situation or universe—appears in that space, plays around there, is known by it, and dissolves back into it again. Are thoughts and feelings the same as mind or are they different from it? They appear from it, play around there, are known by it, and dissolve into mind again, but they behave and are experienced differently. They are like waves in the ocean. Are waves the ocean or are they not?

Recognizing this, we abide in whatever is. We do not get exited when thoughts and feelings arise, do not get sleepy or confused when nothing happens. Just staying in the awareness of WHAT IS, here and now, our mind becomes like a polished mirror: its radiance, intelligence and energy naturally manifests.

The teaching is clear: don't get caught in any of the -isms. If you have materialistic thoughts, don't think that you will never be able to meditate. Just consider them "practical." If you have nihilistic thoughts, don't think you are an incarnation of Nietzsche, but recognize them as such. If you feel idealistic, appreciate and enjoy it without attachment. Whatever arises in mind, manifests its richness, potential and power. But don't identify with it. From resting in that sphere, beyond hope and fear, enlightened awareness will naturally appear.

That is why Hannah and I so enjoy starting centers in the West. In addition to the classical Tibetan and other traditional Eastern styles, an open Western approach is developing for mature, independent people. We are all in the process of making Western Buddhism happen. We, the first generations, are the point of the spear and a BIG shaft will follow. By being honest, constructive and self-reliant now, an inspiring atmosphere will appear and countless fine people will benefit. Being Buddhist means celebrating the fearlessness, spontaneous joy and active compassion of space, and there is no finer thanks to the Buddha and inspiration for others than simply doing our best at this.

The Diamond Way

So Rajgir was the place for the Buddha's "wide" or "inner" teachings on compassion and wisdom. At many times and places, however, a third group of students also came to him. Being artistic and of high energy, these powerful people were inspired by their feeling of closeness to enlightenment. They were unable to see the Buddha as something separate or different from themselves or to help identifying with him. Recognizing his light as the intuitive love which had been growing in themselves for so long, automatically strong devotion arose in them.

Devotion, of course, has many aspects and can lead to many things. Khomeni, Pol Pot, Hitler and Stalin are surely bad, and they could only destroy the massive amounts of happiness and life that they did because of some stupid people's devotion. On the other hand, through the Buddha's example and the words of several Buddhist teachers, many have become enlightened, liberated, or at least they have had meaningful, conscious lives. As devotion is a great force, we should try to understand what it means.

My idea is that devotion is actually recognition. Seeing something which is close to one's own inner nature, one cannot help being inspired. After all: one sees one's own face. If somebody has devotion to a tyrannical dictator, he is thus open to his own hatred, while devotion to a Buddha means identifying with kindness and enlightened insight. So it is not the feeling of devotion we must question, it is its object. There is a difference between devotion to a Mullah or a Lama.

When people had this openness and trust, the Buddha taught the Diamond Way. He showed them their own Buddha-nature. Transforming his body into pure shapes of energy and light, he empowered his students to give enlightened feed-back to their own bodies, to awaken deep psychological responses. The vibration of mantras transmitted his blessing for enlightened speech, and he perfected this work by placing a virus in the neurosis-programs of their minds. This was done through the ultimate teaching called the *Mahamudra*. Here, he shared his insight in such a direct, simple, non-dualistic way that few could forget it. Taking part in the Buddha's realization from the level where seer, thing seen and act of seeing are not separate, many were profoundly changed. As their mental processes became more spontaneous and effortless, they felt happy and at home in every situation. From this first introduction, it was only a question of when the last veil would fall from their minds (see *Mahamudra: Boundless Joy and Freedom*, 1992).

So this is an overview of the Buddha's outer, inner and secret teachings, the Theravada, Mahayana, and Diamond Ways. He must have felt deeply satisfied about his work, for at his death about 2,550 years ago, he stated that he could die happily: He had given all the methods to benefit beings. Since that time, people have worked with this richness of information in three useful ways.

Practical View of the Teaching
Intellectual Approach Prevalent in Institutions

If you visit monasteries or libraries which contain the Tibetan *Kanjur,* you will probably find the teachings arranged in four groups of 21,000 each, depending on their content. One group is called *Vinaya* and works with attachment. It contains especially the rules for monks and nuns, and aims to help people not get caught up in the world. The *Sutra* part changes anger and ill-will, and the *Abhidharma* transforms confusion and unclear thinking. Obtaining these three teachings is like going to school, and only gradually does the information move from head to heart and change us. The fourth group is different: it's like riding a fast motorcycle or falling deeply in love. It is called *Vajrayana* or Diamond Way. If one wants to use the word *tantra* for the part of it involving imagination and form, one must say "Buddhist" tantra. The Hindus also have a tantra, but though the symbolism is often similar, both way and goal are different. If one gets these systems mixed up, one will develop a head like a watermelon, full of unconnected ideas, and a heart like a hazelnut, small and hard.

This fourth group of teachings truly makes us great. It uplifts our view of the world, taking us from the viewpoint of the poor man, of either-or, to that of a rich man, to an all-encompassing both-and. In the Diamond Way one catches the mole of the ordinary mind. One puts contact lenses on its eyes, ties wings to its paws, binds feathers to its tail and sends it into the air like an eagle. Transcending narrowness, everything manifests fresh and new, as the free play of mind.

Over the years, several of my students have become professors of Tibetan or Buddhism at universities, and of course I'm glad about that. I am even more glad, however, when I see that they are now able to live and die better, that they will surely be reborn better, maybe even through mastering consciousness-transference, the famous Pho-Wa. To reach that goal, however, the intellectual overview of the teaching already presented is not the most effective. Much more useful is the practical work. This can happen on three levels, according to the student's wishes and capacities.

Today, three kinds of people come to learn, and they fit the same categories as during the Buddha's time. Probably, however, their proportions are now reversed. Twenty-five hundred and fifty years ago, many liked the general teachings on cause and effect. Fewer wanted the compassion-wisdom teachings, and very few were open to the absolute instructions on the nature of mind. Today in the West, where we are gifted with so much good karma, it seems the opposite. Many want to know about the mind, while people gladly leave cause and effect to the police, to whether one got caught or not. Also, as to psychology and philosophy, we often got too much of it in school. It doesn't turn us on too much, either. Modern people prefer direct experience.

Unity of the Three Levels

Actually, all three kinds of teaching are needed: those bringing about one's own benefit; those developing compassion and wisdom for the benefit of others; and those leading to a direct identification with enlightenment. Each of these three levels consists of three "pillars." To begin with, there must be information. Whichever level one wants to work on, one must first know the situation. Included here is the chance to check what one has heard. Whether we want a life with little trouble, a rich inner experience, or a close and exiting identification with Buddhahood: information and questioning are always indispensable.

In the middle position comes meditation. This pillar is also indispensable. Understanding must become experience, ideas fuse with feeling. After removing obstacles and obtaining right view, merely letting mind come to peace brings about naked awareness and direct growth.

The third pillar consists of holding on to what we have reached. Nothing is less useful and convincing than wearing a big smile one day because life makes sense, and then appearing all depressed the next because nothing works. There needs to be a kind of cementing action, a help to stay with whatever is attained and not to lose it again.

THE NATURE OF MIND

Practical Buddhism

We can thus see Buddhism as a system of nine categories. To benefit egotists, altruists, and yogis, the three levels of students, we have the three pillars of information with questioning, of meditation to obtain experience, and of vows to keep the level attained. I will use the numbers 1 - 9 in the next discussion to make this structure clear.

1. At the first level—with the people who think mainly of themselves—the necessary information is about cause and effect. They need to know what brings happiness and suffering; how to use body, speech and mind for benefit and not for harm. What makes other religions so boring is all their moralizing. You have probably heard enough about things to avoid, so here instead is the Buddha's advice about what to do.

It is wise to consider our body as a tool for protecting others, for giving them the love and material things that they need. The advice about love, of course, does not apply to nuns and monks. On the level of speech, the goal is to calm beings, to show them the world, to make them understand each other, and help them be aware in their life-situations. Concerning mind, his advice was to wish everybody everything good, sharing in the good that they do, and to think clearly, to see cause and effect in what is going on. As our thoughts today become our words tomorrow and our actions the day after, mind is most important.

2. When this is clear, the next pillar is meditation. Its aim on this first level is to pacify the mind, hold it and make so much separation between ourselves and events that we can choose to play in the comedies of life and avoid all roles in the tragedies. This practice often consists of mere awareness of breath, and it is called *Shamata* (Skt.) or *Shine* in Tibetan. When one can hold that distance in the laboratory of one's absorption, seeing changing inner states without reacting to them, gradually one can do the same in one's life. This means really growing up and has great meaning.

3. The methods which prevent downfalls are the so-called outer vows, the ones about what to avoid. In their full extension, there are the hundreds of vows for monks and nuns. On the practical level, they manifest as the essential ones for lay people, such as no killing, stealing, or lying to harm others. Yogis may or may not have vows on this level.

These vows are no Christian or Hindu commandments or Muslim fatwas, religious death-sentences. They can never lead to a situation like that of a Rushdie. We ourselves want the vows. As mature beings, we discover that we are less useful to ourselves and others, when we do, think, or say certain things. That is the reason for the Buddhist vows. The Buddha is never prudish. His view is completely different from that of Muslim or Christian gods. To the Buddha, the body is a temple of light. It contains 72,000 enlightened energies, and there is nothing impure about its parts and functions. The reason for vows is that cause and effect works. Some things we do, think, and say, will bring happiness, while others ripen as suffering. Vows create awareness of that fact.

4. With better feedback from our subconscious and the world around, our mind develops extra dimensions. The energy which is no longer tied up in outer or inner problems expresses itself as compassion and wisdom. Compassion moves through the three stages earlier mentioned and has been perfected when we no longer experience separation between ourselves and others.

Wisdom—the enlightening kind pointing to mind's timeless nature—also manifests as our true essence. It shines forth naturally when the veils of disturbing emotions and stiff ideas have been removed. Experiencing things both as they really are and as they appear, one can benefit countless beings. The many teachings on Bodhisattvahood and emptiness belong here.

5. At this second level, motivation becomes an important part of meditation. We can now start our practice with the wish to get enlightened so we can benefit others. We also end any meditation by sharing all the good accumulated in the process.

6. Finally, to maintain our mental level and keep our inner life rich, we throw out anger. Until a few years ago, this view was far from modern psychology, and certain groups would probably still object. But compare some psychologists or feminists with Buddhists, and you will see which teachings benefit

us most. Really, anger is never useful. Though some insist that all is our parent's "fault" or that of imperialism or society, conveniently forgetting that we make our own lives, anger is a serious mental problem, and is wise to avoid. It makes us lonely and it destroys all our good subconscious impressions. Forceful action without anger, impersonal and motivated by compassion, is much more effective.

Before we get to the Diamond Way, the most exciting part of the teaching, I would like to touch again on some general principles of our Buddhist way and goal.

General Principles of Reaching Enlightenment

Enlightenment is our timeless true nature, and it appears through a very simple process. Just as computers only work with ones and zeros, so also the two steps to enlightenment are repeated again and again. By doing, saying or thinking something positive, mind finds peace. This releases energies which used to be knotted up in tight inner states, and produces experiences of growth. One has space and can see. Recognizing that others are like us, that they also want to be happy and to avoid suffering, how can we deny them that? As we see that they have little control and simply behave as they feel, we must benefit them without judgment.

Thus, the building up of positivity and the resultant wisdom leads to more positivity and more wisdom. Eventually, everything fits. Wherever mind looks, everything is pure. There is only happiness inside and there are only meaningful situations outside. At this point, mind dares to fully step beyond its concepts and experience its clear awareness, its state of timeless clear light.

There is no higher meaning or joy. But of course the ego will soon mix into the process and think: "My clear light was longer than his," or something similar. This doesn't matter, however. If one simply continues, after a while such habits lose their hold. Beyond all fixed ideas, we stay in mind's clear light.

7. Seeing things non-personally and accumulating masses of good then leads to the third level and brings us face to face with enlightenment. Here, the Buddha is clearly no god or person, but a presence that we deeply love and trust. As veils of confusion, mixed feelings, clumsy actions and habits tear away, he becomes something very inspiring and close. At this third level one will develop very quickly. When the conviction has arisen that subject, object, and action are interdependent and really one, reaching the goal is certain.

8. When students of such capacity appeared, the Buddha would give two kinds of meditation. Both are based on identification with enlightenment, on seeing things as naturally pure. We may compare one to a beautiful frame for which people themselves have to make the picture. It is based on the so-called formal initiations. He gave those by either emanating the single Buddha-forms or transforming his own

body into the highest united ones. Manifesting like holograms, these forms are energy and light and correspond to the subconscious potential of various beings.

The single forms were given on the three lower levels of Buddhist Tantra: the Kriya, Charya, and Yoga transmission. Mind's expression on the unsurpassable Mahaanutara Yoga Tantra level are always the united male-female Buddha-forms. Only they are complete. His vase-initiations, touching people's heads and giving them nectar to drink, empowered his students to see themselves as the light-bodies of Buddhas. Making them repeat secret mantras, he awakened their inner energies. In the third initiation, he passed over the power of yogic union, brought together compassion and wisdom, joy and space. The word- or no-word-initiations then planted the ultimate state of Mahamudra in their minds. It gave them timeless insight beyond time and place. Living in a pure land and hearing any sound as mantra, seeing all form as pure, and experiencing every thought and feeling as highest wisdom and joy: how can one not have wisdom and compassion? How could one possibly harm others?

This was not a bad frame, and it is transmitted with fine results also today. Using the building-up phase as taught, meditating on the peaceful, united or protective Buddha-forms in front or above, we shift from an impure to a pure world. Entering their vibration-field through mantra and finally mixing them into ourselves again and again, their qualities are absorbed. One day, meditator, act of meditation, and enlightened form are no longer separate. Trying to be "normal" again, to remove the beautiful Buddha-mask one has put on one's face, then isn't possible. The enlightened qualities are now us.

The picture Buddha gives is even more fascinating than the frame. When he shares his experiences directly, giving us what is called the *Mahamudra*, all concepts dissolve. There is no more direct way than that. Here, he empowers those having confidence—which expresses itself as devotion—with the view that will set them free. Transmitting his non-dual experience, he activates that inner wisdom process which makes one authentic. The very insight that not being distracted by thought is much more important than what is being thought, liberates the spontaneous power in everyone. The ocean has more meaning than its waves.

When his teaching is mainly directed at those motivated by desire, we notice the richness of manifestation and call it *Mahamudra* or *Chag Chen*. When it focusses on primarily angry people, the view is mind's self-liberating quality, and the term used is *Maha-Ati* or *Dzog Chen*. Both are tantric or complete methods for transforming body, speech and mind. A third "Sutric" teaching, *Madhyamika* or *Uma Chenpo*, helps confused people especially. It is an intellectual and much slower way.

9. Holding this third level means deciding never to leave the pure realms. This is not just positive thinking. At this point one knows in the marrow of

one's bones that mind is rich—that it is not a white wall where nothing happens if nothing is projected on it, but rather like a light or a shining diamond, something naturally radiant. Mind in its true nature is open, clear, and unlimited. When it recognizes its space-like nature, all fear is lost. Knowing that our essence cannot be destroyed, complete security arises, a resting in oneself. The important insight here is that we are neither the body which gets old, gets sick and dies, nor the thoughts which come and go. What looks through our eyes and listens through our ears right now is radiant space. It is beyond coming and going, birth and death.

At that level of fearlessness, all events are mind's free play. Both birth and death show its richness. No longer are we like people who go to the cinema, hoping for a good film. We now own the cinema. It does not matter if the film is good or bad, what's important is that there are no holes in the screen and that the projector works perfectly.

As the power of mind becomes more prominent than what it projects, all phenomena, outer as inner, become interesting, simply because they happen. At that level, one thinks like this: A week ago I was jealous, then I became angry, and now I'm confused. How interesting! Let's see what comes tomorrow.

Surrounded by so much fearless richness, and doing what is meaningful, we finally recognize that mind is unlimited. This dissolves any wish for exclusive happiness. On the absolute level, everybody's true essence is limitless space. Seen from the relative viewpoints, all want happiness and wish to avoid suffering. All bodies appeared from parents, were nourished by what the farmer grew, were filled with ideas in schools and universities, experienced happiness or confusion through others and so on. Recognizing everything lasting to be the same in everybody, while all that separates us is constantly changing, how can one be an egotist?

Deciding to stay at that level means behaving like a Buddha until we become one. Seeing everything on the level of purity sustains our whole development. If enlightenment is compared to producing something good, we can see the three kinds of production like this: the first is like a factory in some warm country. Everybody runs around, but not much is happening. Ten good people—the good actions of body, speech and mind—try to keep the ten bad people away. The second level would be like a half-mechanized process. Two men have to work together: compassion and wisdom. If they are okay, products will appear. The signs to watch for are here on the inner level. If egotism appears, it means that compassion is weak. If stiff ideas become important, a lack of wisdom is causing trouble.

The highest level would be like a full-automated factory as in Germany or Denmark. You need only one man for full productivity, and there is only one thing to check: do we experience everything on the level of purity? Are we able to see ourselves and others as potential Buddhas? If that is the case, if we feel everything to be rich and meaningful, perfection will manifest naturally as the timeless nature of mind.

Building down from that highest view is very effective. Much faster than constructing the house of enlightenment alone (called *Theravada*) or even inviting one's friends and using the power-tools of understanding emptiness (*Mahayana*). From the building-crane of highest confidence (*Vajrayana*), we lay down the foundation, erect the walls, add the roof, and the house stands.

Mahamudra is like that: it handles everything and gives meaning to all. Starting at a level where massive good accumulations make mind happy to stay with its impressions, the next step is making us non-artificial. In its light, what really happens is simply so much more interesting than any fabrication or dream. With the third stage, the radiance of the experiencer goes beyond that of any experience, and finally no further effort is needed. We are fully integrated with the highest potential of every being and situation. Any activity will automatically benefit everyone.

This is the view of my students and myself, and the way we teach. If one inspires people to identify with the Buddha, the four stages of Mahamudra come naturally.

After the four Buddhist categories of an intellectual overview and the three steps used on the practical level, there is one more approach to the Buddha's teaching. It is for people who are not in a regular connection with a center or a teacher. They only need to know two things:

First, to always be aware of the absolute view. That nothing really exists except the open, clear and limitless state of mind. That only this truly is. Secondly, one has to remember the relative view, the way. On the outer level, this means avoiding whatever brings suffering. On the inner level, it involves developing compassion and wisdom. On the secret level, it is seeing everything as basically and naturally pure. If we can bring the absolute and relative together, we will have meaningful lives and truly grow.

This was a crash course in the Buddha's full teachings from the view of a Kagyu Tibetan Buddhist. Much of what I wrote here was derived from the greatest Lama of the Karma Kamtsang lineage, His Holiness the 16th Gyalwa Karmapa who is our main teacher. Also, Künzig Sharmapa Rinpoche, the red crown lama of Tibet, the senior lineage holder; our first teacher, Lopön Chechoo Rinpoche; the important Kalu and Tenga Rinpoches; and several others have offered inspiration. Having started so far one hundred thirty Buddhist centers around the world during the last twenty years, I have shared with you some ideas to benefit the intelligent and idealistic West. Enjoy.

Hannah and Ole

Ole's main center in the USA is Karma Jigme Ling, 33 Marne Ave., San Francisco, CA 94127. 415-661-6467, Fax: 431-0139.

Other books by Ole Nydahl

Entering the Diamond Way: My Path Among the Lamas
  ISBN: 0-931892-03-1, 256 pages, 16 full color & 60 b/w photos, paperback, $14.95
Practical Buddhism: The Kagyu Path, with Carol Aronoff
  ISBN: 0-931892-63-5, 48 pages, paperback, $5.00
Ngöndro: The Four Foundational Practices of Tibetan Buddhism, ISBN: 0-931892-23-6, 96 pages, paperback, $9.95
Riding the Tiger: Twenty Years on the Road: The Risks and Joys of Bringing Tibetan Buddhism to the West
  ISBN: 0-931892-67-8, 512 pages, 380 photos, paperback, $17.95
Mahamudra: Boundless Joy and Freedom
  ISBN: 0-931892-69-4, 96 pages, paperback, $9.95

Order from: Blue Dolphin Publishing, Inc.
P.O. Box 1908, Nevada City, CA 95959.
Phone: 1 (800) 643-0765 Fax: (916) 265-0787.